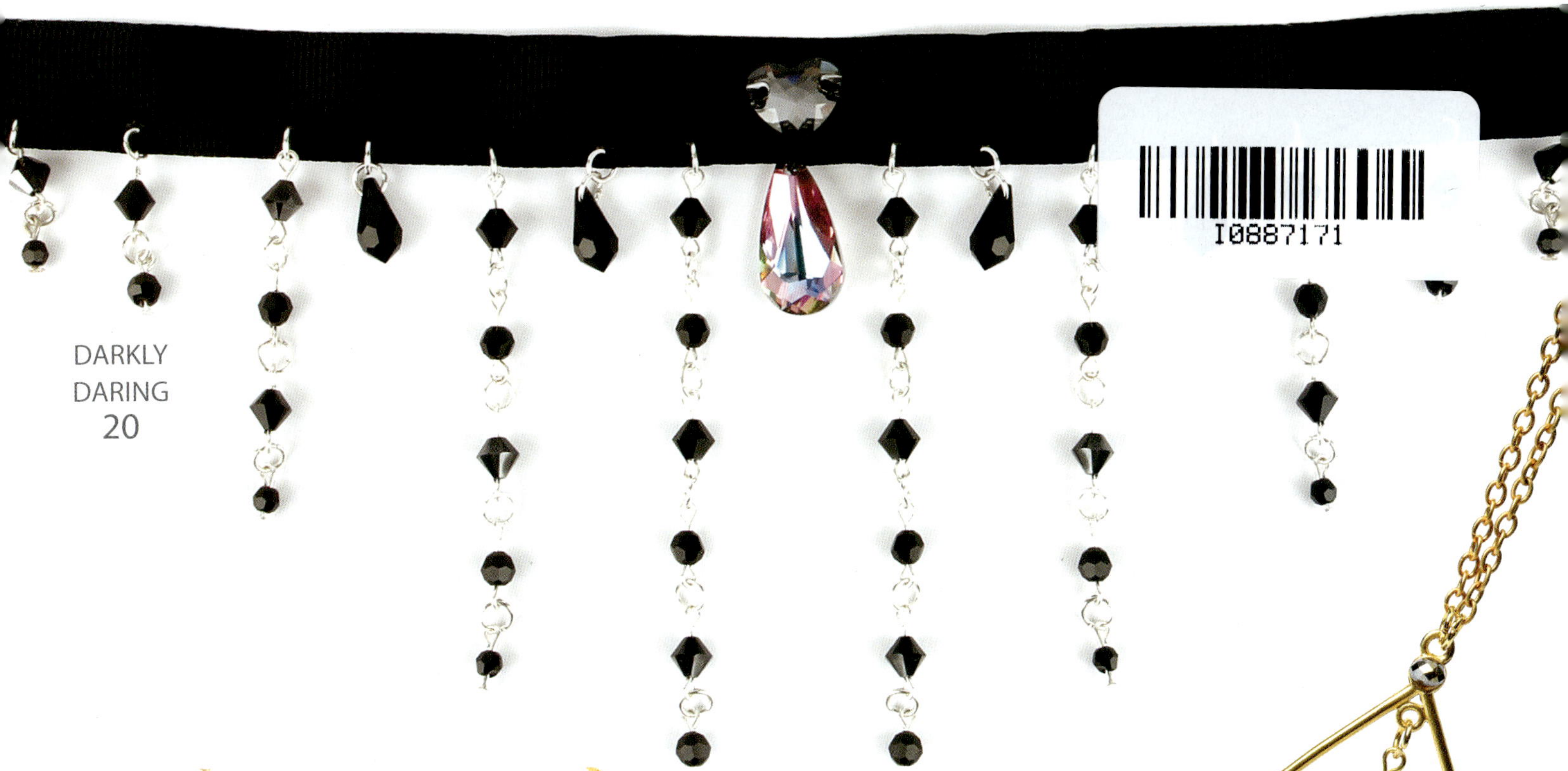

DARKLY DARING
20

TRIBAL PURSUIT
22

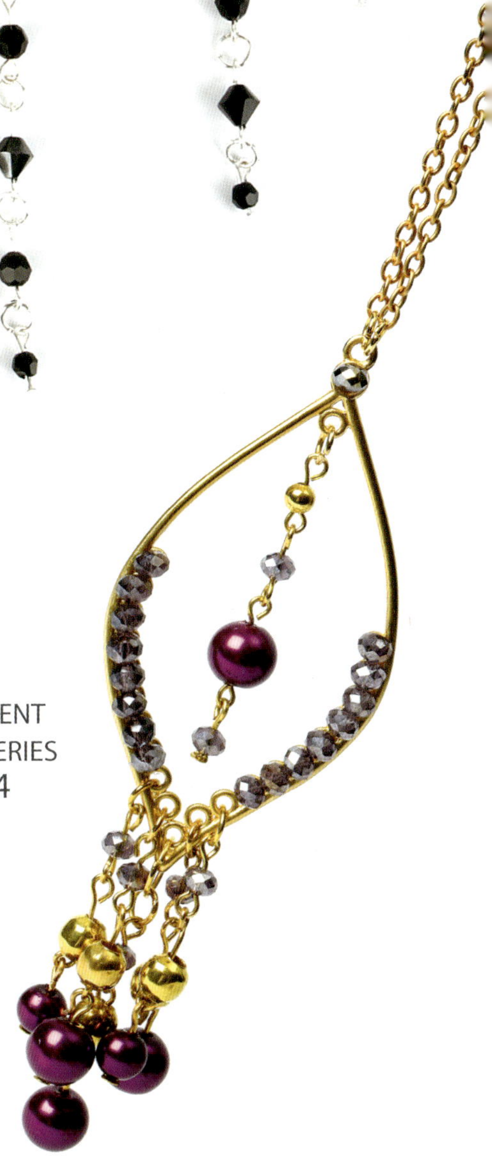

ANCIENT MYSTERIES
14

Produced by GMC Publications Ltd.
86 High Street, Lewes, East Sussex, BN7 1XN, United Kingdom
www.thegmcgroup.com, +44 (0) 1273 477374

MULTIPLE LINKING

By Tansy Wilson

Finding a chain with an unusual link and using a complete mixture of beads that are from the same color palette can create a very effective result suitable for any item of jewelry. Focus on the same joining technique used to attach the beads to give continuity to the design.

MATERIALS

- 9 x Green faceted electroplated 11mm x 8mm drop beads
- 9 x Turquoise mottled 6mm cube beads
- 8 x copper 3mm beads
- 4 x copper daisy beads
- 2 x Green glass 8mm melon beads
- 2 x Turquoise and copper glass beads
- 6 x Green lucite flower beads
- 5 x Jade freshwater pearls
- 1 x copper 20mm toggle clasp
- Copper headpins
- 2 x 5mm copper jumprings
- 20"-24" length of copper chain with small, medium and large links
- Basic jewelry tools

STEP 1

Ensure you cut your feature chain so it is approx. 16"-17" in length but more importantly that it is symmetrical from the center link to either end. Add a 5mm jumpring to each end and before closing them add a toggle clasp bar to one and the actual toggle clasp loop to the other.

STEP 2

Take one of your beads and thread a copper headpin through it. Hold the wire directly coming out of the top of the bead between the jaws of flat nose pliers so the bead is tight to the head of the pin. Bend the wire at a right angle then using round nose pliers at the bend, form an almost complete loop, which looks like a hook.

STEP 3

Thread this hook onto a link on your chain and gripping the back of the hook in a pair of chain nose pliers, start to wrap the excess length of headpin around the upright stalk of headpin coming directly out of the top of the bead. Work all the way down to meet the top of the bead and cut away any excess.

Designer tip

- You can keep the symmetry of your design by mirroring the order of how you attach the beads to each corresponding opposite link.

PHOTOGRAPHS: LAUREL G=UILFOYLE, TANSY WHEELER

STEP 4

Repeat Steps 2 and 3 to continue adding a completely random selection of beads to the medium links on your feature chain.

STEP 5

With some of the leftover links removed at Step 1, take one and gently pry open the copper linking wire with a pair of pliers.

STEP 6

Add this now opened wire to the middle link on your chain and reclose so you have formed an integral pendant. Add more beads to this hoop to create a central focal point to the necklace.

Extra Project
Make a pair of earrings

Use up any extra links of necklace by utilizing them to make into earrings. Remove any linking wire to obtain two matching hoops. Make an earring hook out of a copper headpin and before fully forming it, add a turquoise cube bead. Add onto the eye of the earring hook a 3/8" length of copper chain and one of your large links and close. Add a selection of beads onto headpins and wire one onto the end of the chain and one onto the bottom of the large link. Repeat for the other earring.

BEAUTIFUL CLUSTERS

By Tansy Wilson

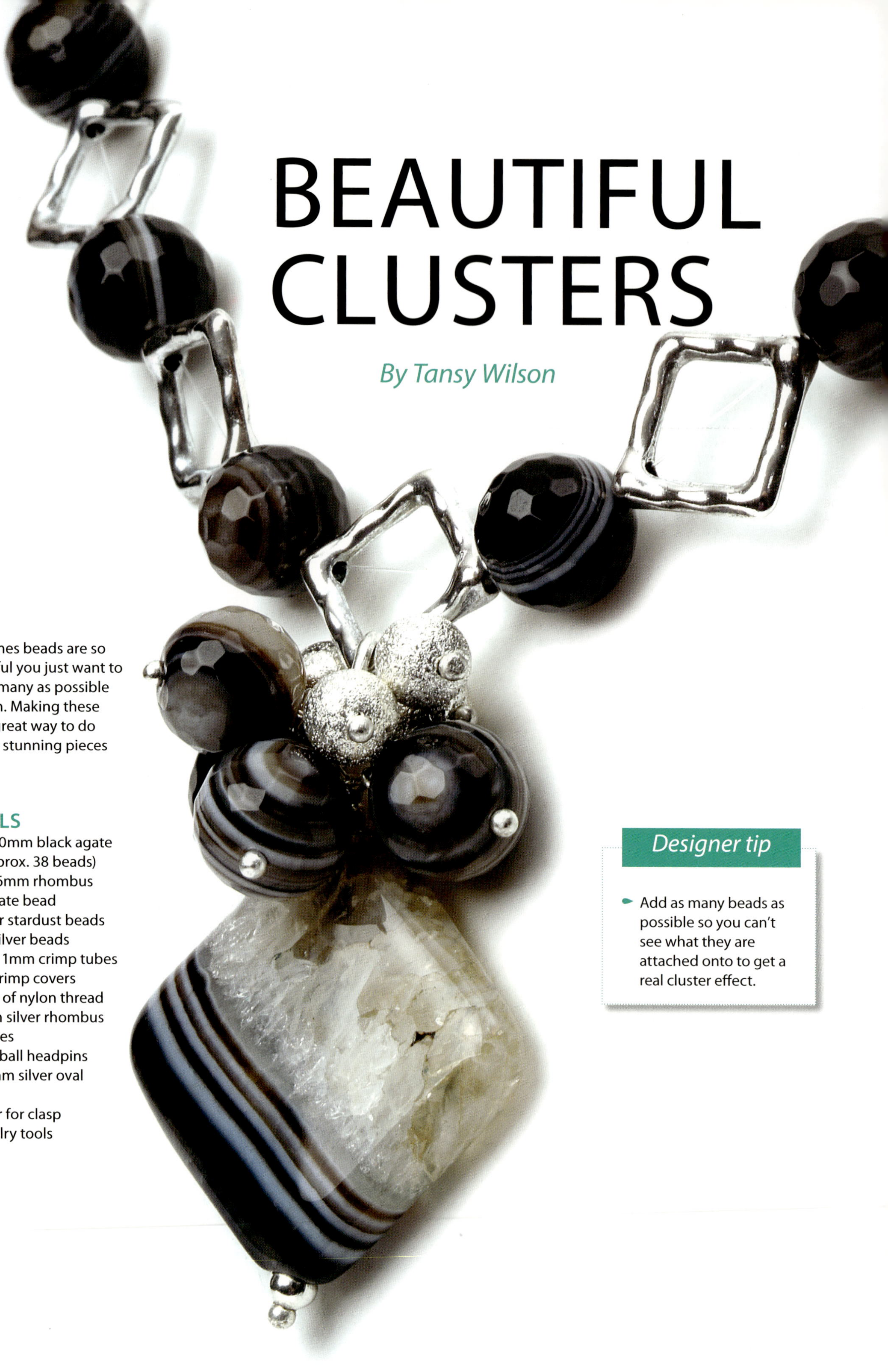

Sometimes beads are so beautiful you just want to use as many as possible in one design. Making these clusters is a great way to do this, creating stunning pieces very easily.

MATERIALS

- String of 10mm black agate beads (approx. 38 beads)
- 16mm x 16mm rhombus striped agate bead
- 6mm silver stardust beads
- 2 x 3mm silver beads
- 2 x 1mm x 1mm crimp tubes
- 2 x 2mm crimp covers
- 16" length of nylon thread
- 12 x 16mm silver rhombus bead frames
- 10 x silver ball headpins
- 9mm x 4mm silver oval jumpring
- Toggle bar for clasp
- Basic jewelry tools

Designer tip

- Add as many beads as possible so you can't see what they are attached onto to get a real cluster effect.

STEP 1

Thread a crimp tube onto a 16" length of nylon thread and pass one end through a rhombus bead and back through the crimp tube. Slide the tube up the nylon so it rests against the rhombus bead leaving approx. 14" length and a 2" tail. Crimp the tube using crimping pliers and add a crimp cover keeping the nylon thread sticking out the bottom.

STEP 2

Thread a combination of agate, stardust and rhombus beads onto the nylon, also threading the 2" tail through the first few beads added. Ensure your design has a rhombus bead at the center. My necklace is 16" long. Thread a crimp tube onto the nylon and pass through the toggle bar and back through the tube. Crimp the tube and add a crimp cover.

STEP 3

Thread a 3mm silver bead onto a headpin and then thread the headpin through your agate rhombus bead. Add another 3mm bead and make a wrapped loop at the top. Open the oval jumpring and link this agate focal bead to the center rhombus bead of the necklace.

STEP 4

You can now add as many beads as you like to form the pendant cluster with your focal agate bead. Thread headpins through a selection of agate and stardust beads and make a hook at the very top of each one.

PHOTOGRAPHS: LAUREL GUILFOYLE, TANSY WHEELER

STEP 5

Take one hooked bead and thread the headpin through the wrapped loop made at the top of the focal agate bead. Hold the stem of the hook in your pliers and wrap the remaining excess wire from the headpin around the stem securing it on. Repeat to add a bead to the other side of the loop.

STEP 6

Continue adding as many beads as you like to the oval jumpring. Add them both at the front and back of the jumpring to achieve a large tight cluster.

Extra Projects
Make earrings and rings

This method of clustering beads can be used to make a matching pair of earrings. It can also look very effective when used in other designs too. Add lapis lazuli and gold beads to a looped ring for this stacked up effect or try adding bead cups to these turquoise beads for a more layered silver and blue cluster effect.

MAGICAL SPACE

By Clair Wolfe

Use several simple jewelry making techniques to create this magical and meaningful necklace.

MATERIALS

- 7 x Sterling silver pierced bead caps
- 3 x Sterling silver blank ovals 1.5mm thick
- 7 x Sterling silver blank open flower charms
- 63" of Sterling silver navette trace chain
- Sterling silver navette trigger clasp
- 4mm and 5mm heavy Sterling silver jumprings
- 7 x Triangle Sterling silver jumprings
- 30" of 20 gauge (0.8mm) Sterling silver round wire
- 7 x 8mm Sea Green round faceted lucite beads
- 7 x Crystal shards/points
- Basic jewelry tools
- Nylon mallet
- Ball-peen hammer
- Hammer
- Steel block
- Newsprint lowercase letter punch set
- Hand drill
- Black permanent marker
- Nail polish remover
- Soft cotton cloth
- Masking tape
- Scrap polymer clay
- Center punch
- Emery paper or file

STEP 1

Take two pairs of flat nose pliers and a triangle jumpring. Open the triangle jumpring with the same twist motion used on a round jumpring. Push one side of the triangle into a crystal shard and then carefully close the triangle jumpring; this may take a little time and careful manipulation. Once closed, use a nylon mallet and steel block to harden the jumpring.

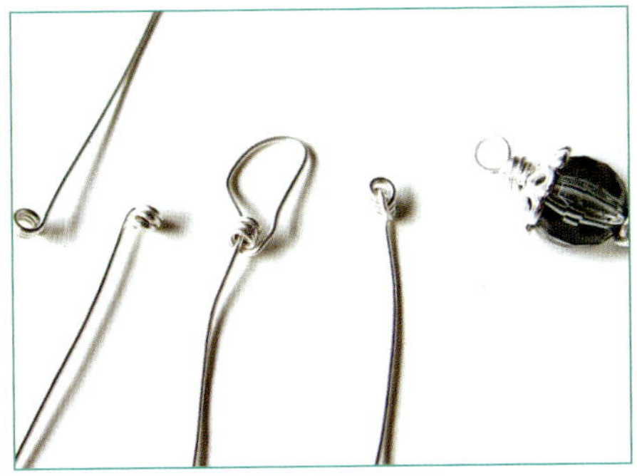

STEP 2

Cut ten 3" lengths of 20 gauge wire. Take one of the lengths and use the tip of round nose pliers to grasp one of the ends. Begin to create a coil with two or three turns. Bend the remaining wire up across the coil. Bend the wire so that it can be threaded through the coil. Use pliers to pull the wire though as tightly as possible. Use to make 7 beaded drops with the bead caps and 8mm beads.

PHOTOGRAPHS: LAUREL GUILFOYLE, CLAIR WOLFE

STEP 3

Press the blank oval into a scrap of clay to practice letter spacing and to see if your chosen inspirational words will fit on the blank. Use a strip of masking tape to secure a blank to a steel. Position the first letter on the blank and strike with a hammer. Repeat this with all letters from your chosen word.

STEP 4

Use a center punch and hammer to create guide holes for a drill. Use a drill to complete holes on either side of each oval blank. Turn the blank over and use emery paper or a file to remove any burrs that have been formed by the drill.

STEP 5

Take a permanent marker and work the color into the stamped letters on the blank. Allow to dry. Add a little nail polish remover to a soft cloth and wipe over the surface of the blank to remove any excess ink. Repeat, inking on any area that needs a little more definition. Lightly texture the surface of the blank with a ball-peen hammer.

Designer tips

- Use clay to check the orientation of each letter before stamping.
- Add words that hold a personal meaning to you.
- Add further lengths of chain for a more extravagant finish.

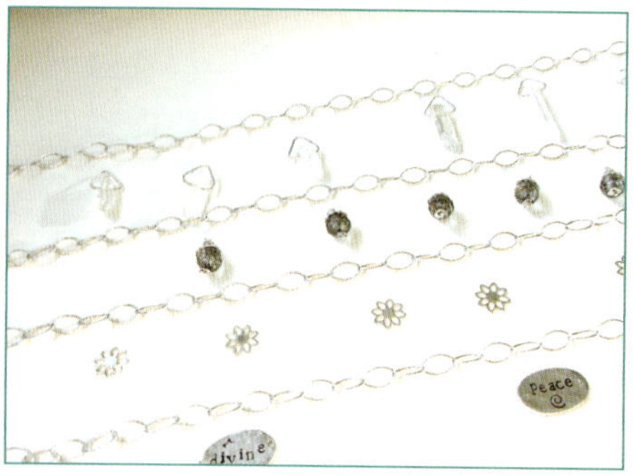

STEP 6

Cut four lengths of chain: 12", 14", 16" and 18". Lay them out so that the 16" length becomes the base for the necklace design, then the 12", the 14" and the 18". Experiment with the placement of the crystal shards, the beaded drops, the stamped ovals and a selection of silver flower charms.

STEP 7

Once happy with the positioning of the stamped ovals, use wire cutters to cut the 12" chain and attach an oval with a jumpring on either side. Do this for all three ovals, making sure that the stamped face is facing forward and is right side up.

STEP 8

Find the center of the remaining three chains and then using a jumpring, add a crystal shard, a flower charm or beaded drop to the chains. Work your way out from the center, equally spacing the positioning of all the attachments.

STEP 9

Add your clasp to the 16" chain. From the last link on the chain, count in the same number of links from each side. Use a sturdy jumpring to attach all three chains to this point on the main chain. Try the necklace on to make sure that all the chains sit nicely, if not move the chains, repeat until happy with the overall look.

Extra Projects
Make earrings and a bracelet

EARRINGS

Create simple matching earrings by adding a selection of chain, flower charms and beads to a pair of earwires.

BRACELET

Thread a selection of beads onto a short length (6") of beading wire; finish both ends with a crimp bead. Add a stamped oval to one and then a clasp and the second part of the clasp to the other end. Use jumprings to add a selection of beads and flower charms.

ETERNAL BRIAR

By Gill Teasdale

Gothic style is a dream to work with, allowing for the use of fun elements and daring colors. This necklace favors the trend's more feminine side and has a hint of romance using ribbon, crystal droplets and a sleeping beauty element represented by the eternal briar connector of thorns, alongside more dramatic components.

MATERIALS

- 8 x silvery eternal briar metal connector
- 16 x 4mm antique silver filigree round beads
- 6 x antique silver tiny daisy spacers
- 11 x 2" antique silver eyepins
- 32 x 5mm antique silver jumprings
- 10 x 7mm antique silver jumprings
- 8 x 5.5mm silver-plated bead caps
- 2 x (8mm x 8mm) silver-plated ribbon end clamps with teeth
- 67"of 1" black organza ribbon
- 4 x 4mm and 4 x 6mm Swarovski Elements Siam rounds
- 3 x 11mm Swarovski Elements Siam pendant drops
- 10 x 11mm Swarovski Elements Jet pendant drops
- 3 x 14mm Swarovski Elements Crystal Silver Night cross bead
- Basic jewelry tools

STEP 1

Open the eye on an eyepin, hook onto the loop on a briar and close. Thread a filigree bead, a 4mm Siam and a filigree bead, make a loop, and hook onto another briar loop before closing. Repeat with three more beaded eyepin links, making a chain of five briars. Join the bottom of the briars with four more eyepin links beaded with a filigree bead, a cap, a 6mm Siam, a cap and a filigree bead. Bend each eyepin into a curve.

STEP 2

Cut four 2-link pieces of chain and two single links. Using a 5mm jumpring attach a 2-link length to the bottom left loop on the top second left briar, attach a 1-link to the right loop. Using two separate jumprings attach both chains to the loop on a new briar. Do the same on the middle briar using two 2-link chains and the next briar using a single link then a 2-link.

STEP 3

Hook a 5mm jumpring onto an eyepin and then onto a Siam drop. Slip a daisy spacer, a cross bead and a daisy spacer onto the eyepin. Make a wrapped loop. Hook onto a 5mm jumpring then hook the jumpring onto the bottom loop of one of the newly attached briars (it will be hanging diamond-wise). Repeat twice.

PHOTOGRAPHS: LAUREL GUILFOYLE, GILL TEASDALE

STEP 4

Attach 7mm jumprings to all the jet drops, hang one on each outside bottom briar and one on each side of the middle bottom briar. Working on the top row briars hang two on the bottom of the center briar, one on the right loop on the left briar, one on the left loop on the second left briar. Complete the right side to match.

STEP 5

Cut two 17-link, two 13-link and two 6-link lengths of chain. Using 5mm jumprings hang a 17-link between the top and middle left briars and the other between the top and middle right briars. Hang a 13-link between bottom left and bottom center and the other between the bottom center and bottom right. Hang a 6-link between middle of bottom left and middle of center and the other between the middle of center and middle of the right briars.

Designer tips

- Careful bending of the eyepins will create a gentle curve around the necklace.
- If ribbon is not your thing, it can easily be replaced with heavy chain or leather.

STEP 6

Cut the ribbon in half. Take one end, fold the edges into the center, then into the center again. Place between the jaws of a ribbon clamp and squeeze the teeth together to grip the ribbon. Slip a 5mm jumpring onto the loop on the clamp and the remaining loop on the left of the top row of briars. Repeat for the other side. Cut a "V" in the ends of the ribbon.

Extra Project Make earrings

EARRINGS

For earrings, simply hang a briar with a Siam round suspended inside, from a fishhook. Hang three chains from the remaining three briar loops, bringing them together with a jumpring and mini cross charm.

PARIS IN THE FALL

By Joan Gordon

Use pretty charms from your favorite cities to remind you of your travels. The charm can also be a favorite animal, flower or general shape.

MATERIALS

- 8 x 12mm crystal multi-faceted beads
- 9 x 8mm multi-faceted beads
- 16 x brass bead caps
- 20" fine link brass chain
- 17 x 2" brass eyepins
- 4 x vintage or similar charms
- 6 x 4mm brass jumprings
- 1 x 4mm split ring
- 1 x bronze lobster clasp
- Basic jewelry tools

STEP 1

Set out on a work mat the eight 12mm crystal beads. Thread a bead cap onto an eyepin followed by a crystal bead and then another bead cap. Using flat nose pliers bend the extending metal of the eyepin into a right angle bend. Snip the pin down to approximately 1/4". Grip the end of the pin in the jaws of round nose pliers and roll the wire into a neat secure eye. Repeat this step for all eight beads.

STEP 2

Thread an 8mm crystal bead onto an eyepin. Make a simple loop at the end of the pin. Repeat for all nine beads. Set aside four 12mm beads; these are to be decorated with chain. Cut from the length of chain four lengths each approximately 1 1/2" long. Open the eye at each end of a 12mm crystal and link the eye through the end links of the cut chain. Securely close each eye with bent nose pliers. Repeat this step for all four beads.

STEP 3

Cut two 1/2" lengths of chain and link one end of each length to the eyes at either side of an 8mm crystal bead. Open a jumpring and link one free end of chain onto the ring followed by a metal charm and then the other free end of chain. Close the ring securely. Open the eyes at one end of two 12mm crystals and link these carefully to the eyes extending from either side of the center 8mm crystal; these three linked beads form the center of the necklace. Close all the eyes and check that the charm drops neatly at the front.

PHOTOGRAPHS: LAUREL GUILFOYLE, JOAN GORDON

STEP 4

Make two charm drops using 1" of chain joined to a jumpring and the top of each charm. Working from the center of the necklace out to each side, open the eyes at either end of the 12mm linked crystals and add an 8mm crystal to each open eye. Close to secure the 8mm crystals. Open the extending eyes from the 8mm crystals and carefully link each charm drop. Before closing the eye, link a 12mm crystal decorated with chain to either side.

STEP 5

Measure and cut two 5" lengths of chain (more if desired) that will link either side to the front focal beads. On each side of the center of the necklace add two 12mm crystals that aren't decorated with chain, separated by 8mm crystals using the eyepins to connect them. To finish, link a final 8mm crystal to a link on the free end of both lengths of chain then secure this link to the 12mm beads at either end of the crystal linked necklace.

STEP 6

Attach the lobster clasp to a jumpring and link this jumpring to the free end of the connecting chain. To the other side of the necklace add a split ring to the end link of chain. This split ring acts as a closure that connects with the clasp. To further enhance the necklace link a small length of chain to a jumpring, attach this to the split ring and connect a small charm to the free end of chain to hang from the back of the necklace.

Extra Project Make crystal earrings

CRYSTAL EARRINGS

Thread a bead cap followed by a 12mm crystal, another bead cap and an 8mm crystal onto a 2" long headpin. Form a single wrapped loop at the top of the headpin. Link the wrapped loop to the eye at the base of a fishhook earwire. Repeat to make the second earring.

ANCIENT MYSTERIES

By Jaide Lillie

This stunning pendant necklace is the perfect piece to pair with a caftan on the beach or even to a glamorous garden party. Using rich and vibrant colors inspired by an Indian summer, this necklace is a look anyone can pull off!

MATERIALS

- Gold-plated findings: Clasp, headpins and eyepins
- 6mm Fuchsia round glass pearls
- 8mm Fuchsia round glass pearls
- Crystal faceted 4mm rondelle purple violet AB beads
- 6mm Gold-plated spacer beads
- 4mm Gold-plated spacer beads
- Gold-plated brass chain
- Medium dreamcatcher pendant
- Super glue
- Basic jewelry tools

STEP 1

Create five accent drops for the medium pendant. Use a headpin for the first pearl and loop, then add on a 6mm gold spacer, a crystal bead and a jumpring – connect them all using looped eyepins. Three drops should start with 8mm pearls and two should start with 4mm pearls. Attach the drops, using a large jumpring for the center drop so that it hangs lower than the rest.

STEP 2

Create the centerpiece for the pendant. Use a headpin for a crystal bead and loop, then add on an 8mm pearl, a crystal bead, a 4mm gold spacer and a jumpring - connect them all using looped eyepins. Using the jumpring, add to the loop at the very top of the pendant.

STEP 3

To add the crystal detailing use super glue (or you can wire wrap these to the pendant frame with a thin wire if you prefer). Use a headpin and insert down the nozzle of the tube. Add small dots of glue to the edges of the outer and uppermost loops and carefully place your crystals using pliers. Be careful not to get glue on any visible crystal.

PHOTOGRAPHS: LAUREL GUILFOYLE, HOLLY BAXTER

STEP 4

Set the pendant aside for five minutes to allow the glue to dry. Give the pendant a gentle tap on a tabletop to make sure the crystals have been placed correctly. If any drop off, repeat the process. Attach two 10" lengths of chain to the top loop of your pendant using two jumprings. Go through all loops in your piece and ensure that they are all closed flush.

STEP 5

Hold the pendant and chain up to you as though you were wearing it, and check how the length sits on you. You may wish to shorten the chain at this point to make the pendant rest higher up on your chest. Simply measure and snip off if required. When you are happy with the length of your necklace, use two jumprings to attach to either end of a toggle clasp.

STEP 6

The frame of this pendant is very versatile and at this point you can continue adding on more pendant drops or crystal accents. Continue adding on beaded drops to the center, or you could even try wire wrapping a delicate design across the body of the pendant to create a dreamcatcher effect with crystals scattered throughout. Wrap wire through the frame in zigzag motions, travelling upwards, and then back through.

Extra Projects Make earrings and bracelets

EARRINGS

Make smaller versions of the pendant using smaller dreamcatcher pendants and findings; attach three dangles instead of five. Attach to earwires with jumprings.

BRACELETS

Use any leftover beads to create simple matching bracelets by stringing onto elastic. Simply knot when you are happy with the lengths and secure with a dab of glue. Trim any excess elastic and they are ready to wear!

Designer tips

- You may wish to purchase a 1-Step Looper® for this project; it will make looping all your pieces together much easier.
- Flat nose pliers work best when placing your crystal beads onto the pendant frame to glue in place.

ROSE GOLD

By Clair Wolfe

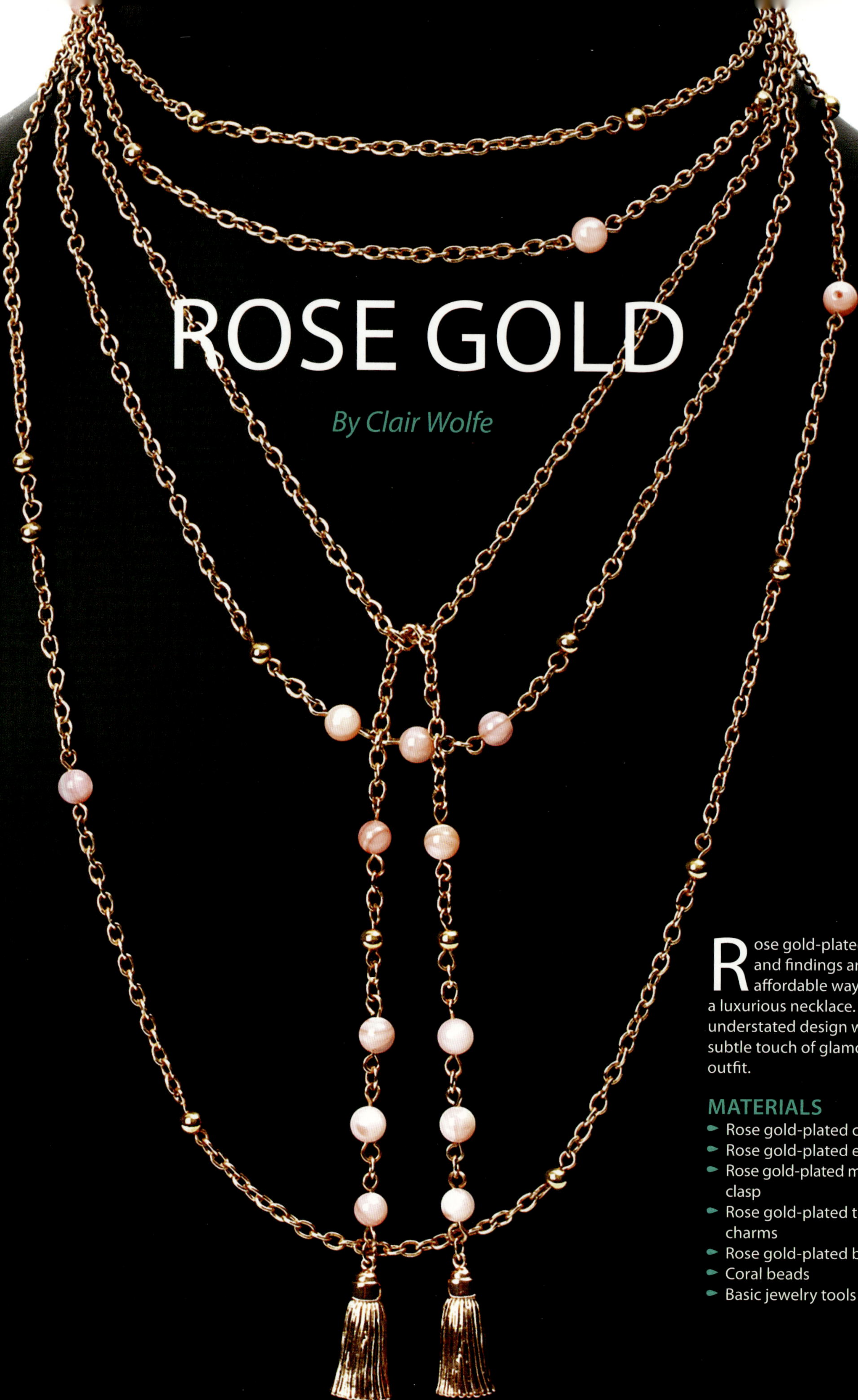

Rose gold-plated chain and findings are an affordable way to create a luxurious necklace. This understated design will add a subtle touch of glamour to any outfit.

MATERIALS

- Rose gold-plated chain
- Rose gold-plated eyepins
- Rose gold-plated magnetic clasp
- Rose gold-plated tassel charms
- Rose gold-plated beads
- Coral beads
- Basic jewelry tools

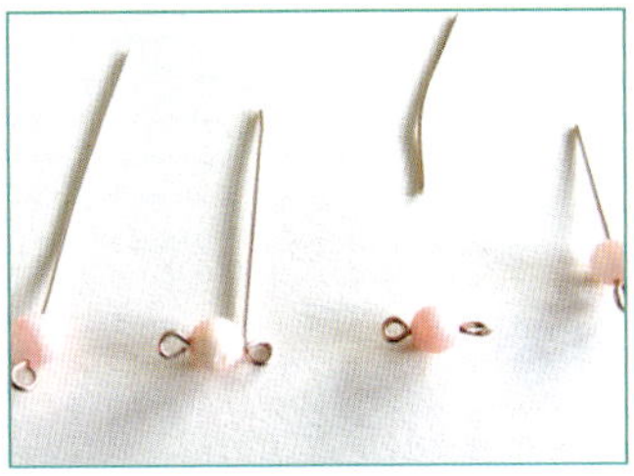

STEP 1

Thread a coral bead onto an eyepin until it sits above the eye. Use a pair of round nose pliers to create a loop at the other end of the bead. Use wire cutters to cut away the excess wire, neaten the loop with a pair of chain nose pliers.

STEP 2

Cut three lengths of rose gold-plated chain, one $14\frac{1}{2}$" and two 17". Use a jumpring to attach one end of the $14\frac{1}{2}$" and one of the 17" chains to one half of a magnetic clasp. Use a twist motion to open and then to close the jumpring. Repeat on the second side of the $14\frac{1}{2}$" chain and 17" chain.

STEP 3

Find the center point of the $14\frac{1}{2}$" chain and use two pairs of pliers to open one of the chain links; once again use a twist motion. Use this link to attach one of the wired beads, and open a link on the other side of the chain; use this link to attach to the second side of the wire bead. Add a selection of beads onto the chain along the length.

STEP 4

Remove a short length of chain from each of the long chains and open up each of these links. Use these links to add a number of beads to each of the long chains. Finish with a rose gold-plated tassel on each side.

PHOTOGRAPHS: LAUREL GUILFOYLE, CLAIR WOLFE

STEP 5

For an alternative design, take a second length of rose gold-plated chain and add beads along the length at intervals, once again by opening a chain link and adding a bead. Use a final wired bead to join both chain ends together to form a continuous beaded loop. This can be worn doubled up or at full length layered up with the first necklace.

STEP 6

This project is two necklaces worn together. For the second piece make a long chain interspersing rose gold beads and coral beads along the length. Make this chain long enough to wrap three times over your head with out a clasp. If you don't want to have them separate then add more strands of chain to Step 2.
On this page you can see the chains worn separately.

Extra Project Make earrings

EARRINGS

Make two long beaded pieces as in Step 4 and hang from earwires for a lovely pair of matching earrings.

CLUSTER NECKLACE

By Linzi Alford Buckmaster

Handmade polymer clay charms are added along with beads to a chain length. You can make it as clustered as you wish by adding more dangles. Use the same technique with different colorways for endless variation – why not make one for each season?

MATERIALS

- 24" bronze curb chain
- 4 x acorns and leaves polymer clay charms
- 1 x toggle clasp
- 9 x 2" headpins
- 9 x 12mm x 8mm glass drop beads
- 9 x 6mm bicone beads
- 8 x 6mm bronze jumprings
- Basic jewelry tools

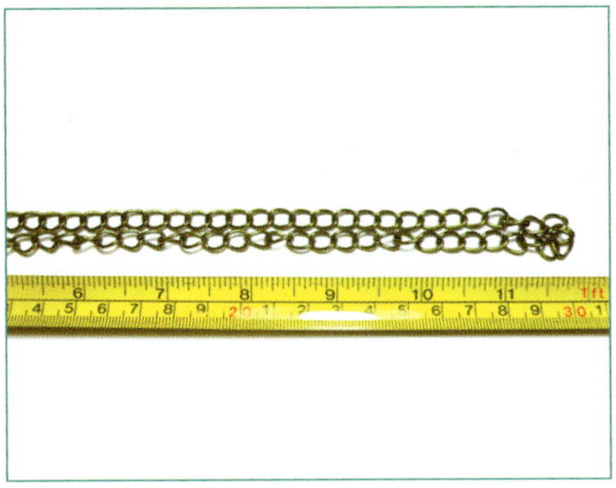

STEP 1
Measure and cut a length of chain to the desired length for your necklace. If unsure place it around your neck to judge where it will sit – allow extra for the clasp. I used 24".

STEP 2
Attach the toggle clasp using jumprings. Offset the toggle (i.e. do not place it at the end of the chain) to add interest. The necklace will then fasten at the front.

STEP 3
To make the bead dangles, thread the 12mm x 8mm glass drop beads and 6mm bicones onto 2" headpins.

STEP 4
Construct wrapped loops on the headpins: make a right angle bend, wrap the wire around the jaws of the round nose pliers to make a loop. Pull the wire around the headpin using bent nose pliers and cut excess off with wire cutters. Tuck the cut end in neatly.

STEP 5
Attach the beaded dangles to the bottom end of the chain beneath the clasp using jumprings. Stagger along the chain links to make them hang nicely.

STEP 6
Using jumprings again, attach the polymer clay charms in between the bead dangles to the chain. Add one leaf to the very end of the chain.

PHOTOGRAPHS: LAUREL GUILFOYLE, LINZI ALFORD BUCKMASTER

Extra Projects Make earrings and a bracelet

EARRINGS
A really quick pair of earrings can be made by simply attaching the polymer clay leaves or acorn charms to earwires using a jumpring.

BRACELET
Cut a length of chain to approximately 7" long and attach a clasp at each end. Add as many bead dangles as you wish plus a central focal polymer clay leaf or acorn charm following the main project steps.

DARKLY DARING

By Jaide Lillie

Step into those dark winter nights with a chic glimmer of Swarovski crystal. This choker is a real showstopper and will go perfectly with a little black dress.

MATERIALS

- 6mm Swarovski bicones
- 4mm and 5mm Swarovski faceted rounds
- Swarovski Vitrail teardrop pendant
- Swarovski sew-on heart stone
- Black grosgrain ribbon
- Ribbon ends
- Lobster clasp (optional extension chain)
- Jumprings
- Headpins
- Eyepins
- Beadsmith 1-Step Looper®
- Basic jewelry tools

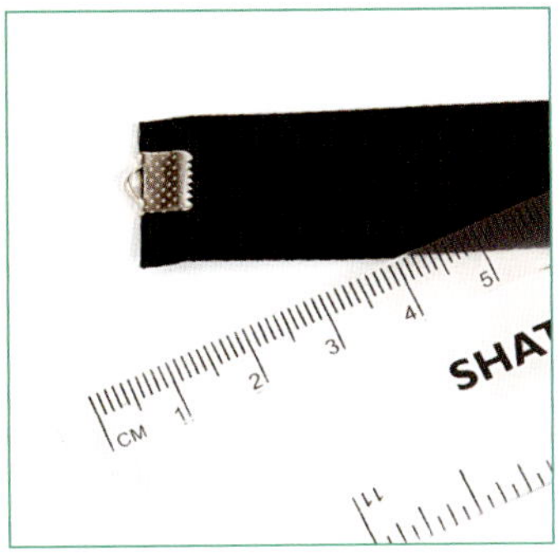

STEP 1

If you are making this for yourself, measure the length of your neck using a piece of string and a ruler. Subtract 1" and cut the ribbon to the length required. Attach a ribbon end flush to each end of the ribbon. Add a lobster clasp and an extension chain (useful if selling your choker or gifting it). Attach using jumprings through holes on the ribbon ends.

STEP 2

Take a Swarovski drop pendant of your choice and a sew-on heart stone. A combination of a light and bright colors works perfectly with a darker color for a stunning contrast of crystals. Stitch both of your Swarovski pieces securely onto the direct center of your ribbon. Make sure you don't pull your threads too tightly when you stitch on the drop pendant; you want a slight amount of movement.

STEP 3

At this stage, start planning out your pattern. Using a variety of 4mm, 5mm and 6mm bicones and faceted rounds, lay out your Swarovski beads in a pattern you want for the decoration. For this design, I have attached four small Swarovski drop pendants at 1" and 2" distances from the center pendants. Try experimenting with a variety of shapes and colors for a different look and feel.

STEP 4

Once you have established the pattern, begin to attach all of the top jumprings onto the ribbon. Leave them open so that you can add on your drops once they have been completed. Aim to punch your holes for the jumprings approx. 1/8"-1/4" from the bottom of the ribbon. Again, make sure you don't force them through as you'll create pulls in the weaves of the ribbon fibers. Be gentle!

PHOTOGRAPHS: HOLLY BAXTER

STEP 5

Attach the Swarovski beads onto eyepins, trimming and looping them. Place them back on your beading mat to keep them in the correct order. (You will find it much quicker to use the 1-Step Looper for this.) Remember to attach the bottom bead (on each of your vertical drops) to a headpin as it doesn't need two loops. Drops look particularly effective in a big bead/small bead pattern.

STEP 6

Once you have looped all of the beads you need for your dangles, you can begin to attach them together using jumprings. Do this dangle by dangle using the pliers in a 'push away' motion, holding the jumpring in place with the other hand to open and close your jumprings without bending them. Once you are happy with the design of your choker, go back through all of your jumprings, headpins and eyepins and double check that they have all been closed completely.

Extra Projects
Make a bracelet and earrings

BRACELET

Use any leftover beads to create a simple crystal bead bracelet using techniques used to create the dangle drops.

EARRINGS

You can also attach a few looped beads onto an earwire for a simple yet effective pair of earrings.

TRIBAL PURSUIT

By Gail Florio

Inspired by tribal trends using feathers around your neck, this extravagant design is stunning when worn but simple to make.

MATERIALS

- Large gold jumprings (8mm–10mm)
- 28" length of hackle feather fringe color 1
- 24" length of hackle feather fringe color 2
- Gold filigree cone ends (19)
- 20 gauge (0.8mm) gold plated copper wire
- 11" thick link gold curb chain
- 10" medium link gold curb chain
- 13" thin link gold curb chain
- 12" gold chain
- Small beads (3mm–6mm)
- Lobster clasp
- 78" suede cord
- Basic jewelry tools

STEP 1

Cut a 2½" length of feathers from your feather fringe, gather together and shake off the fluff (you might want to do this outside or over a trash can). Take a 6" length of 20 gauge wire and wrap around the top of the feathers three times. Tuck the end of the wire into the feathers and leave a long tail of wire protruding.

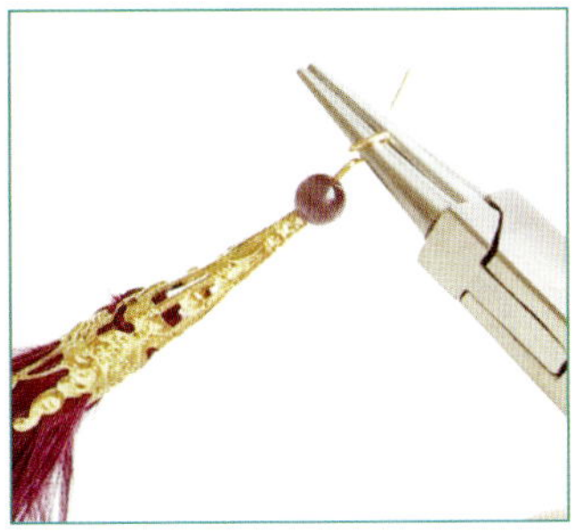

STEP 2

Insert the wrapped feathers into a filigree cone, with the long tail coming out the top. Pull up so that the wrapped wire around the feathers is hidden or blended into the gold cone. Add on a few small beads and create a wrapped loop. Trim off any excess wire. Make a further 18 feather cones, nine in one color and ten in a contrasting color.

STEP 3

Cut three lengths of curb chains: small, medium and large. The top chain (medium) should have 34 links, the middle chain (thick) 23 links and the bottom chain (thin) 66 links. Link together with jumprings by leaving two links apart in the top chain, one link apart in the middle chain and five links apart in the bottom chain.

PHOTOGRAPHS: LAUREL GUILFOYLE, GAIL FLORIO

STEP 4

Cut a piece of suede cord about 78" long. Tie one end into a thick chain link, knot and pull tightly. Weave the cord through the top and middle chains. Each link of the thick chain will have two wraps, and the medium top chain one wrap. Skip a link if the top chain is becoming too far away from the middle chain to have neat wraps.

STEP 5

Visualizing the bottom (thin) chain as grouped sections separated by jumprings, add a feather cone to the third link of each grouped section. The nine main colored feather cones will be placed along the bottom chain. Add the remaining ten (secondary color) feather cones to the jumprings connecting the top and middle chains. Your secondary color should hang on top and in between the main color.

STEP 6

Decide how low or high up you would like your necklace to sit and cut another piece of gold chain at an appropriate length. On one side, connect to the middle chain using a jumpring and on the other side, add a clasp. Add an additional jumpring to the middle chain for the clasp to secure in to.

Extra Projects
Make earrings and a necklace

EARRINGS

Following Steps 1–2, make up two feather cones. Attach to gold earring wires using small jumprings.

SINGLE FEATHER NECKLACE

Using 5"-6" of feather fringe, follow Steps 1–2 to make a feather cone. Attach to a length of chain (long or short) using a jumpring. Add a clasp to finish off.

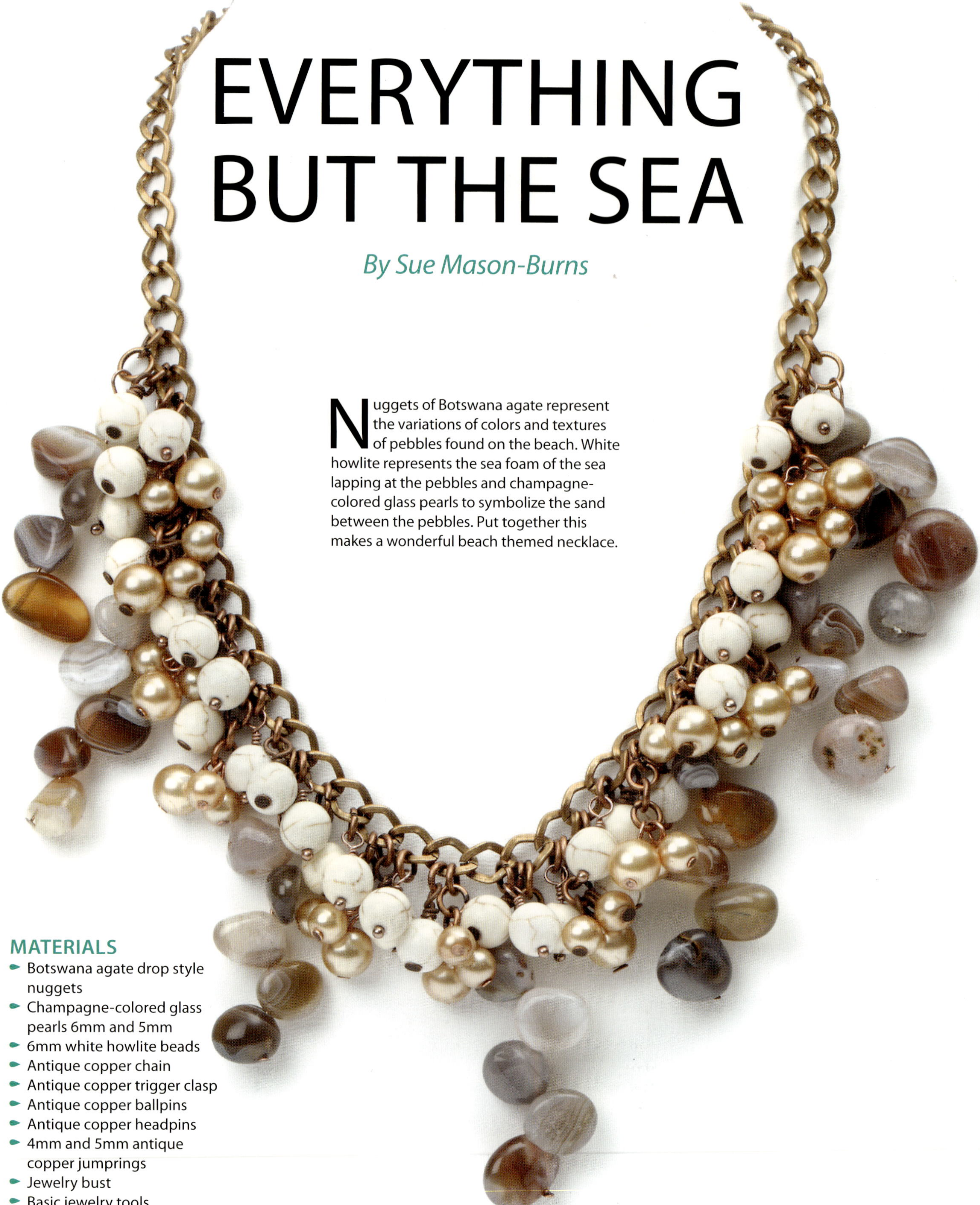

EVERYTHING BUT THE SEA

By Sue Mason-Burns

Nuggets of Botswana agate represent the variations of colors and textures of pebbles found on the beach. White howlite represents the sea foam of the sea lapping at the pebbles and champagne-colored glass pearls to symbolize the sand between the pebbles. Put together this makes a wonderful beach themed necklace.

MATERIALS

- Botswana agate drop style nuggets
- Champagne-colored glass pearls 6mm and 5mm
- 6mm white howlite beads
- Antique copper chain
- Antique copper trigger clasp
- Antique copper ballpins
- Antique copper headpins
- 4mm and 5mm antique copper jumprings
- Jewelry bust
- Basic jewelry tools

STEP 1

Cut a length of chain long enough to sit just on the collarbones of the wearer. Use two pairs of chain nose pliers to open a 4mm jumpring, remembering to open the link away from you, rather than pulling it apart, as this will weaken the jumpring. Thread on a trigger clasp and link onto the last link of the chain. Close the jumpring.

STEP 2

Thread howlite beads onto a mixture of ballpins and headpins and complete wrapped loops as follows: leave a gap of approximately 1/8" and use chain nose pliers to bend the pin to 90 degrees. Take the wire of the pin around round nose pliers to form the loop. Coil this wire around the pin above the bead until the gap is covered. Trim the pin.

STEP 3

Repeat Step 2 until you have enough howlite beads to cover all but 8" of the chain. Hang the chain on a jewelry bust and begin attaching howlite beads to every link with 4mm jumprings, alternating the ballpins and headpins as you go. Start in the center and alternate sides as you add to ensure symmetry. Leave the last 4" of chain bare on each side.

PHOTOGRAPHS: LAUREL GUILFOYLE, SUE MASON-BURNS

STEP 4

Thread five agate nuggets onto a headpin and finish with a simple loop: bend the headpin to 90 degrees directly above the bead. Trim the headpin to approximately 1/2" and use round nose pliers in a rolling motion to form a loop, ensure that it closes flush with the top of the bead.. Open a 5mm jumpring and thread through the loop of the nugget dangle. Close the jumpring. Make 7 of these dangles. Use a 5mm jumpring to attach the nugget dangles to the chain at regular intervals, beginning in the center. Add the final nugget dangles to the first link of the bare section of chain.

STEP 5

Thread two 5mm and one 6mm glass pearls onto a headpin and finish with a simple loop. Make 12 of these dangles.

STEP 6

Open a 4mm jumpring and thread on the three pearls, with the 6mm in the middle. Close the jumpring. Open another 4mm jumpring and use this to attach the cluster of pearls onto the chain, behind the howlite beads, and in between the agate, ensuring that they sit below the howlite. Add further 4mm jumprings if necessary to gain the right length.

Extra Projects Make earrings and a bracelet

EARRINGS

Thread two teardrop shaped beads onto headpins and make a simple loop. Thread two bead caps and champagne-colored glass pearl beads onto eyepins and make a loop. Link the loops together and add earwires.

BRACELET

Thread Botswana Agate faceted rice beads onto eyepins and link together with 7mm jumprings. Thread 5mm champagne-colored glass pearls onto eyepins with a bead cap and make a simple loop. Attach six pearls to the 7mm jumprings, three either side of the beads. Attach a toggle clasp.

SUNBURST

By Laura Binding

The beauty of this necklace is that it can be made in any color combination and can be worn as a daytime look and still make the easy transition to a stunning evening piece.

MATERIALS

- 26 gauge (0.4mm) silver plated wire
- Silver plated trace chain
- Yellow chalcedony briolettes
- Fire opal briolettes
- Moonstone briolettes
- Silver plated metal rondelle beads
- Silver plated findings
- Artistic Wire® Coiling Gizmo®
- Basic jewelry tools

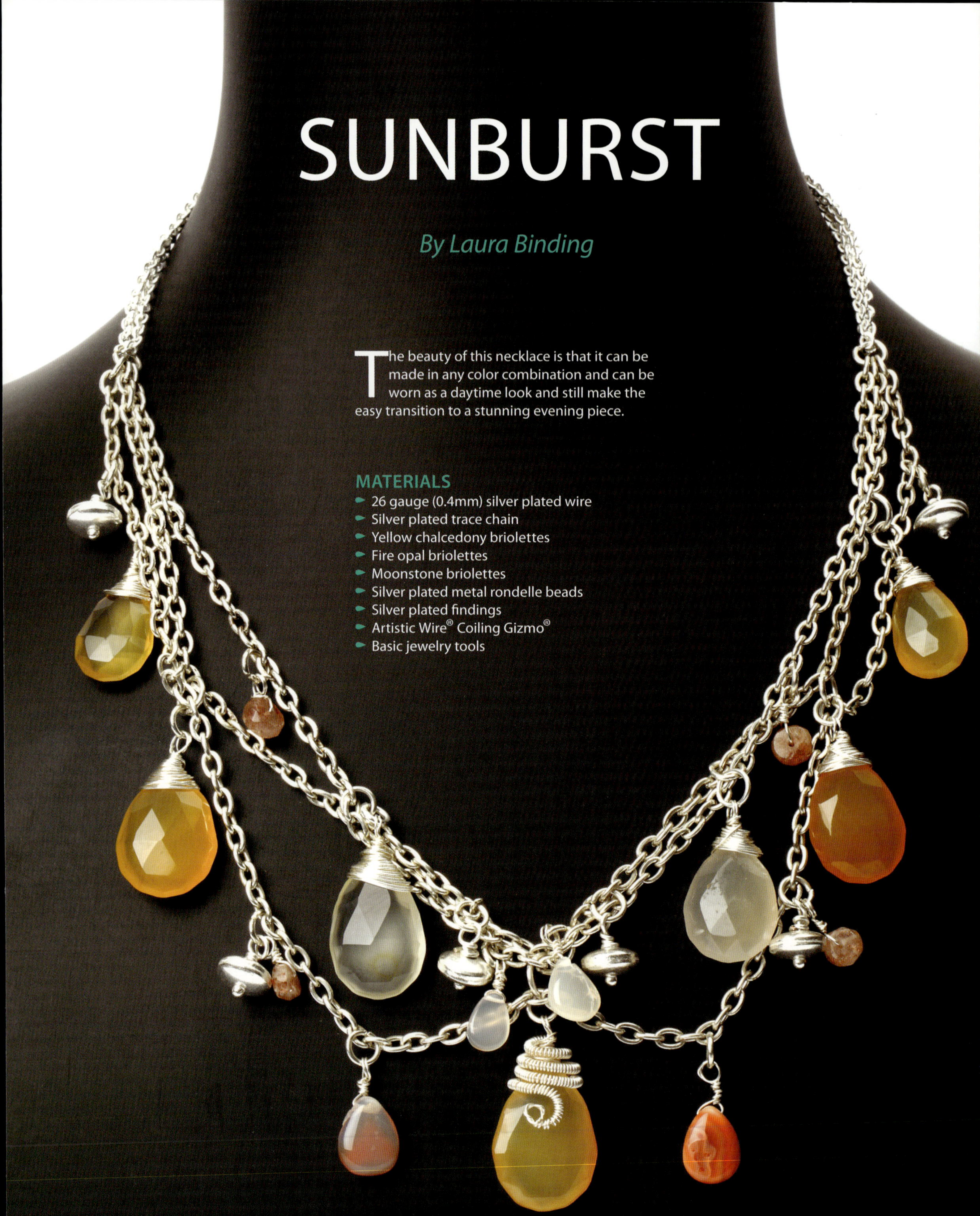

STEP 1

For the focal stone, use 26 gauge wire and keeping it on the spool, thread the wire through the top of the briolette and leave a small tail. Twist the two wires together and cut the excess wire off the short end of wire.

STEP 2

Take your round nose pliers and place them at the top of the twist, hold the wire with your pliers and wrap the wire around the pliers once, and then open the pliers slightly and make a second wrap.

PHOTOGRAPHS: LAUREL GUILFOYLE, LAURA BINDING

STEP 3

Continue to use your pliers to hold the piece firmly and bring the wire around to the twist at the top of the stone and wrap it to secure the loops. Slowly start to wrap the wire down the twist and to the top of the stone, then keep wrapping slowly and bring the wire around the top of the stone.

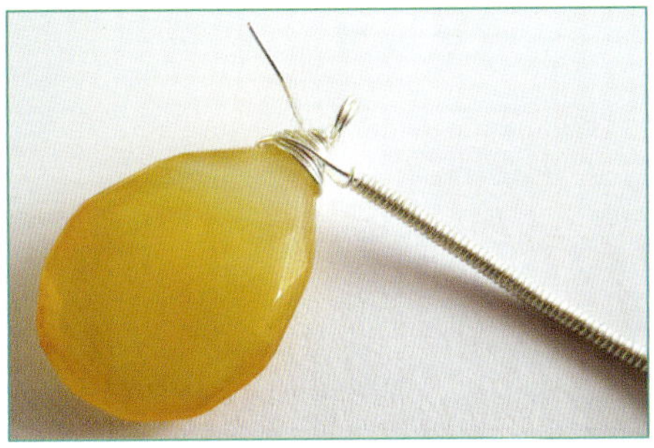

STEP 4

Leave about 20" of wire and cut from the spool. Use 26 gauge wire and create a small separate coiled gizmo section about 4" long. Keep a tail on the gizmo section and put the gizmo wire onto the excess wire from the stone and secure the tail around the top of the stone. Wrap the coil around the stone spiral and twist the ends together to secure.

STEP 5

Cut three lengths of chain, 16", 18" and 20", add jumprings onto all three chains so you have a three tier necklace. Lay the necklace down and find the center of all three chains; thread a large jumpring through the center link on the chains and add the focal stone. Cut two more 16" lengths of chain. Thread a chain length through each jumpring on the necklace. Use a jumpring to add a clasp to the loose chain ends.

STEP 6

Once you are happy with the position of the focal stone, lay the necklace out again, wrap more stones and position them where you would like them to hang. Attach them to the links on the chain with jumprings. You can catch one or two chains together and leave them with just briolette drops or add even more texture by adding little drops of smaller stones and metal beads.

Extra Projects Make a pendant and earrings

PENDANT

Create a simple pendant by just wrapping a large stone and adding it to a decorative toggle clasp. When finishing plain briolette wraps bring the wire back to the top of the wrap and cut flush, then squeeze with pliers to remove sharp edges.Make this the feature of the necklace.

EARRINGS

To create cluster earrings, add a stone to a piece of chain and add two stones per link.

BRING ON THE BLING

By Karen Caine

Use a variety of leftover beads to build this bursting and bubbly statement piece.

MATERIALS

For one cluster bead

- 12" of 18 gauge (1mm) soft wire
- 36" of 20 gauge (0.8mm) soft wire
- 8" of 0.38mm tiger tail (needs to hold kinks)
- 12 x assorted beads (3mm–10mm)
- Approx. 6 x crimp beads
- Approx. 3 x crimp covers
- Seed beads for flourishes (optional)
- Basic jewelry tools

For necklace

- 24" of tiger tail
- Clasp
- 2 x crimp beads
- 2 x clamshell bead tips
- 56 x 4mm beads

Designer tips

- If the cluster beads keep turning on your necklace to reveal the backs, consider linking them together with S-shaped spiral links rather than simple tiger tail or create 3D versions of the beads by adding more prongs and having them face in multiple directions.
- You can add buttons, lace flowers, spikes or anything else to your design that takes your fancy.

PHOTOGRAPHS: LAUREL GUILFOYLE, KAREN CAINE

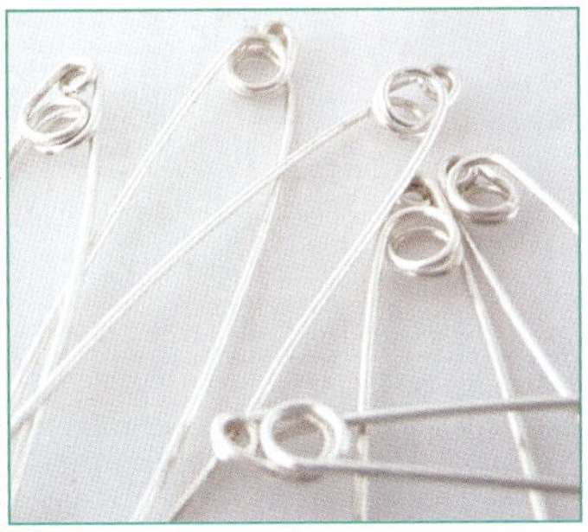

STEP 1

Start each cluster by cutting six 6" lengths of 20 gauge wire. Take one of these wires and make a loop in the middle using the round nose pliers. Move the pliers and create a bigger loop on one of the straight lengths, right next to the loop you just made. Flip the piece over and do the same on the other side. Repeat for all the pieces of wire to create six prongs.

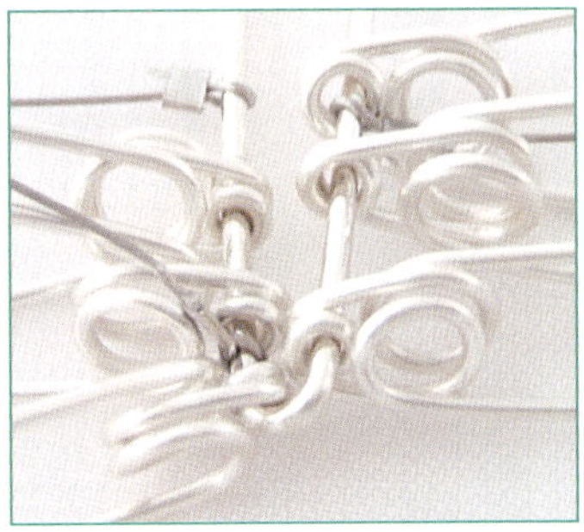

STEP 2

Cut three $2^{3}/_{4}$" lengths of tiger tail and one 12" length of 18 gauge wire. Fold the 18 gauge wire in half, then slide a prong onto each half of the 18 gauge wire. Use a crimp to add a piece of tiger tail to one side. Repeat three more times, adding the tiger tail to alternate sides.

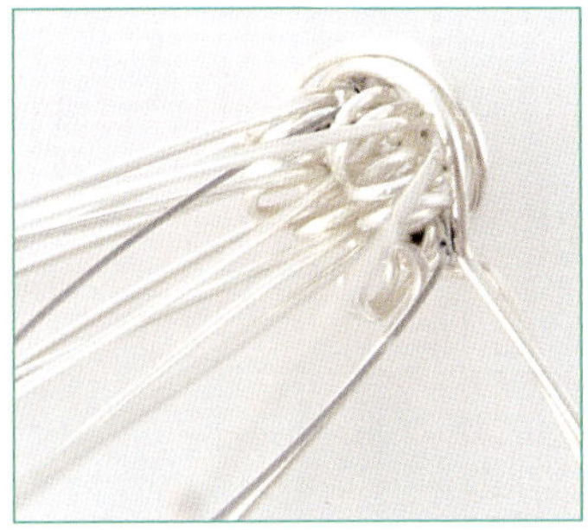

STEP 3

Make sure the prongs are all pointing in one direction, then wind the left end of the 18 gauge wire round to the right to complete a circle, then do the same with the right end, crossing it over the left end to lock it in place. Repeat this three times, ensuring that the wire that starts at the bottom, finishes at the top on each half-turn. Bend the wires to run parallel again.

STEP 4

Add beads in whatever way you choose. I use larger beads to provide a base and then add smaller ones on top. I've also chosen a simple color scheme with lots of shapes and sizes, but feel free to experiment. Once the beads are in position, lock them into place by spiraling the ends of the prongs and flattening them against the bead.

STEP 5

Once you have beads on all the wire prongs, you can add them to the tiger tail. You can fill up the whole length if you wish, but I like having a crimp bead and cover just on the tip and then coil the tiger tail around the round nose pliers. It gives a wonderful arcing curl that reminds me of fireworks and party poppers. It also gives the piece a sense of movement.

STEP 6

To turn the cluster into a bead, make two spirals with the 18 gauge ends and flatten them into the back. You can then string them together for any project by threading your stringing material through the big loops you created in Step 1. For a necklace, choose loops one third of the way from the top, so that the bead doesn't hang face down. You can check how it lies using a jewelry bust.

Extra Projects Make a brooch and a ring

BROOCH

Create a fun stick pin brooch by spiraling one of the 18 gauge ends and flattening it against the back of the bead. Then trim the other end to 2" and file it to a sharp point. Add a pin protector and it's done.

RING

Create a funky, size-adjustable cocktail ring by changing Step 6, so that you wrap the two 18 gauge ends around a ring mandrel (or pen), taking the ends either side of the cluster bead to form an open ring. Curl the wire tips into small spirals.

BASIC TECHNIQUES

HOW TO MAKE A WRAPPED LOOP

1. Thread a bead onto a headpin or eyepin. Grip the wire with round nose pliers next to the bead.

2. Bend the wire above the plier jaw to a right angle. You will need about 1/8" of wire above the bead before the bend.

3. Move the plier jaws to sit at the top of the bend.

4. With your thumb push the wire back around the pliers, keeping it tight to the jaw.

5. Keep pushing the wire around the jaw until you meet the bead.

6. Move the pliers around the loop and continue to bend the wire around until it is facing out at a right angle and you have a complete loop.

7. If attaching the loop to a chain this is the stage to do that. Use a pair of chain nose pliers to hold across the loop firmly.

8. Wrap the wire around the neck of the loop until it meets the bead. Snip off any excess wire and push the end against the coil to finish.

MAKING A SIMPLE LOOP

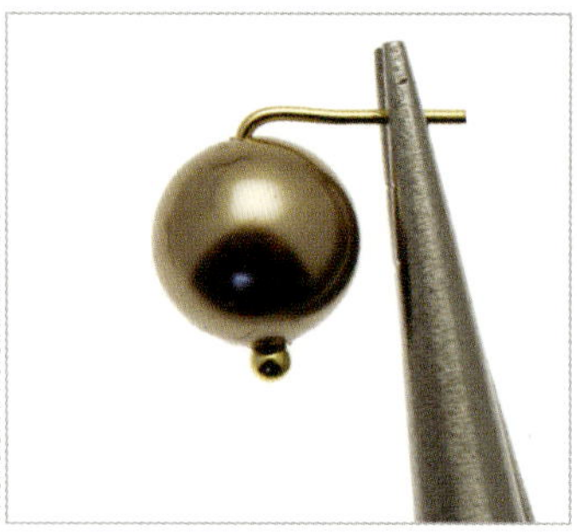

PHOTOGRAPHS: SIAN HAMILTON

1. Thread the bead onto a headpin or eyepin and cut the pin about 3/8" above the bead. Bend the wire to a right angle above the bead.

2. Using round nose pliers, grasp the wire at the very end and curl it around the plier jaws.

3. Roll the wire around to meet the bead. Bend the loop back to sit directly above the bead.

4. Use chain nose pliers to tighten the loop by twisting it from side to side. Do not pull it outwards as that will distort the shape.

USING JUMPRINGS

Always make sure you follow this guide and don't pull jumprings apart as they can easily distort.

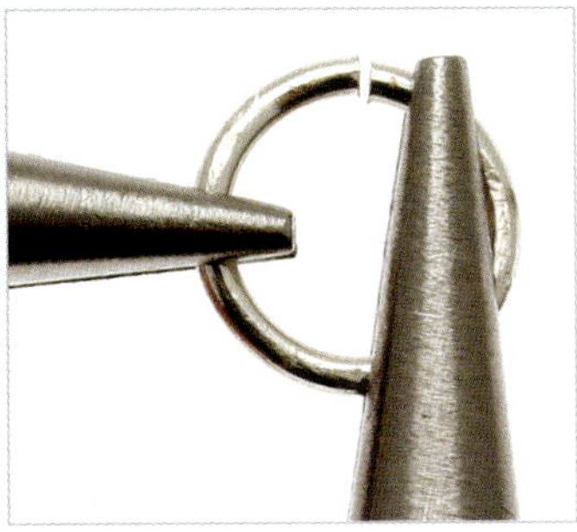

Take a jumpring in two pairs of pliers with the opening centered at the top.

Hold the jumpring either as shown in the step above or this step.

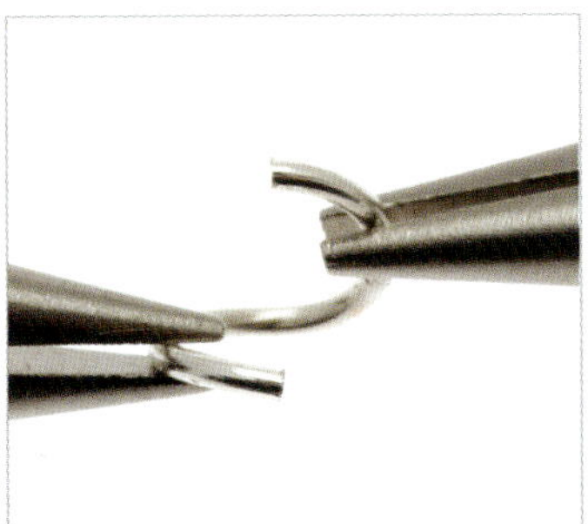

Whichever way you hold the jumpring, the opening motion is the same. Twist one hand towards you and the other hand away; never pull apart. Reverse the action to close.

CRIMPING A BEAD

To show this process clearly it is being shown without using thread; the thread or wire should be inside the crimp bead.

Hold the crimp bead in the pliers with the bead in the hole that has a round side opposite a 'W' shape.

Before closing the pliers, check that the bead is straight. When you close the pliers the thread or wire should fall either side of the bend.

Move the 'U' shape crimp to the other hole with two round sides. Turn the crimp so the 'U' faces sideways and press the pliers closed tightly.

ADDING A COVER

Crimp covers make your finished jewelry look more professional and clean.

Take a crimp cover and place it over the crimped bead, making sure the bead is completely inside the cover.

Take a pair of chain or flat nose pliers and carefully grasp the cover. Gently press the cover closed.

The finished cover should be closed into a perfect bead shape. Nylon nose pliers do this job very well as they won't mark the cover.

MAKING AN EYEPIN

Make your own eyepins using 20 gauge (0.8mm) wire. You can use 18 gauge if you need strong pins.

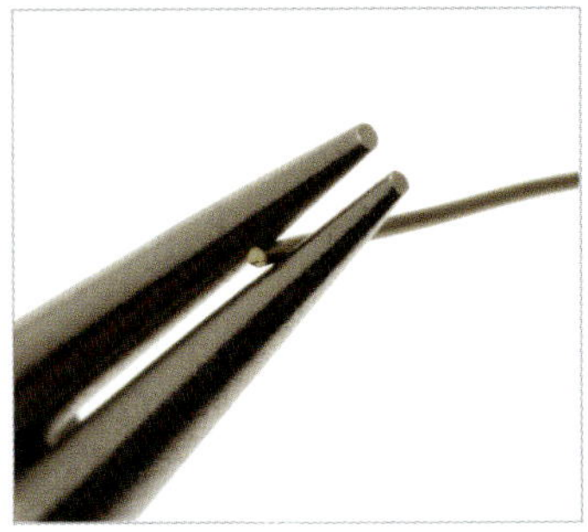

Take the very end of the wire in round nose pliers. If the wire is quite hard it may slip out of the pliers, so start the loop about 1/8" in and snip off the straight piece as you make the first curve.

The shape you want to create is a P. The advantage to making your own eyepins is that you can make the loop any size you need.

To finish the pin so the loop sits centered on the wire, take the round nose pliers and place them where the round P shape meets the wire. Press the wire back against the pliers until the loop is centered.

BASIC TOOLS

TYPES OF PLIERS

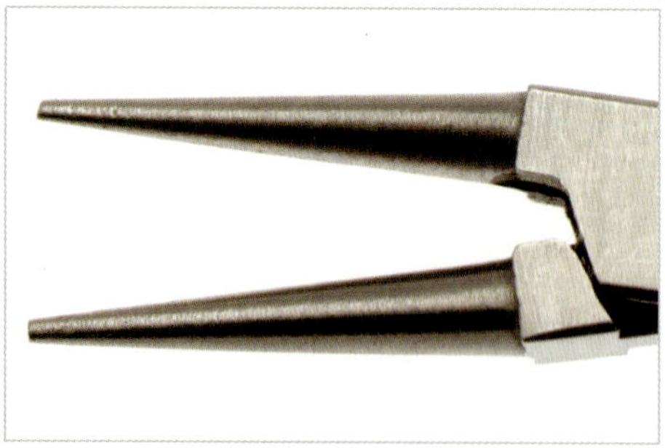

ROUND NOSE

These are a must-have for a basic kit. When making jewelry, being able to create loops and rings is essential.

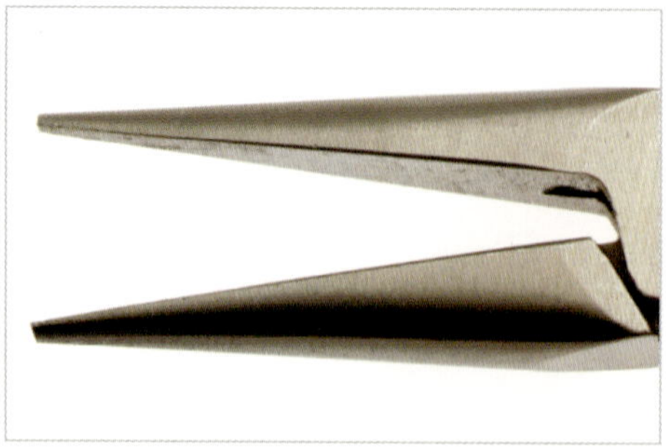

CHAIN NOSE

Also called half round, these are the most versatile. They are used for many jewelry applications, so are another must-have for the basic kit.

FLAT NOSE

Similar to chain nose, these pliers have a wider jaw that is completely flat. Good for holding jumprings/findings as the wide jaw grasps a large area.

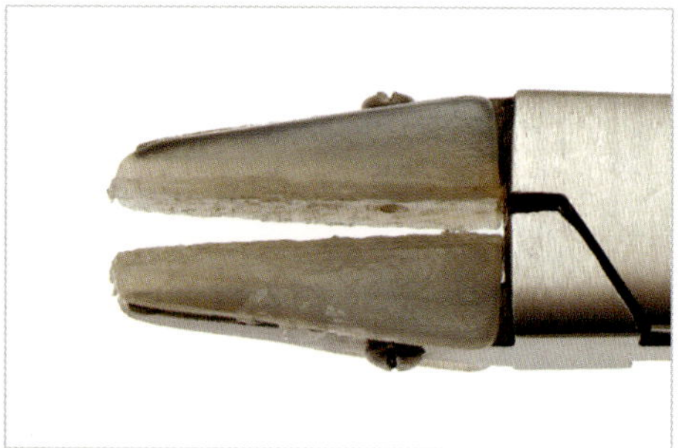

NYLON NOSE

Another similar style to flat nose, these pliers have jaws that are covered in nylon to stop them marking the metal.

BENT NOSE

Used for getting into small tricky spaces where a straight nose pair cannot reach.

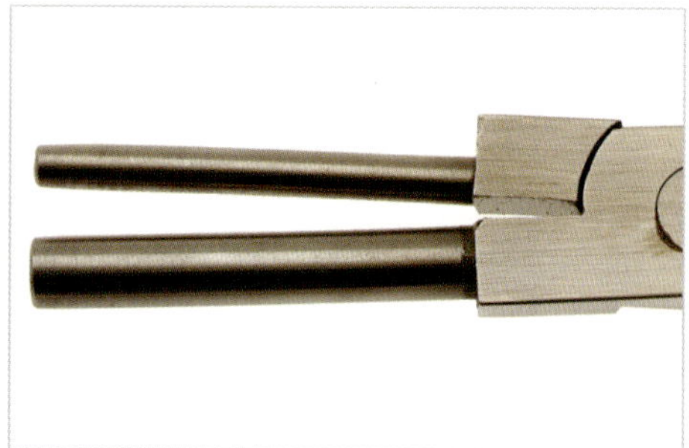

BAIL MAKING

These pliers have fixed sized jaws, with each jaw being a different size, usually with a 2mm difference (such as 3mm and 5mm). They come in a wide variety of sizes and are great if making a lot of the same size jumprings or coils.

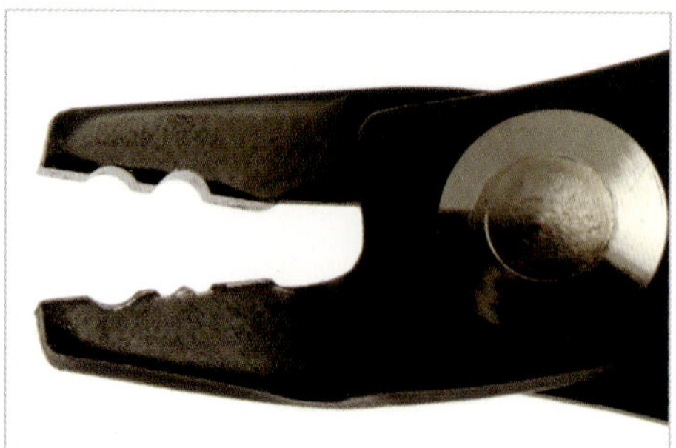

CRIMPING

These pliers are used with crimp beads. If you want to have a nice finish to your crimping then these pliers are a good investment.

WIRE CUTTERS/SNIPS

These pliers are also called side cutters. They come in a vast range of prices and styles. Be careful what you cut as they can blunt easily if used with hard or large dimension wire.

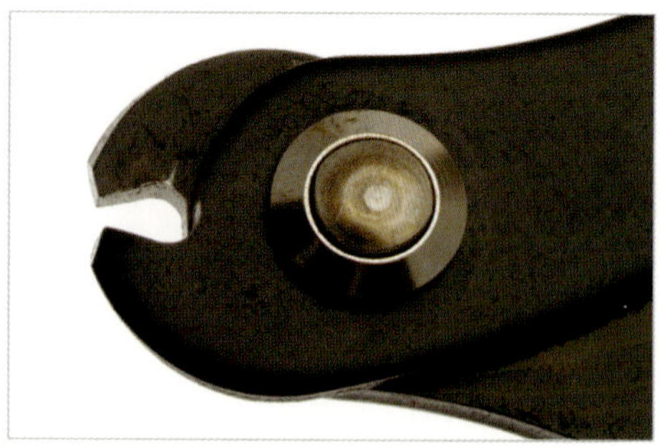

MEMORY CUTTERS

Used exclusively for cutting memory wire. If you are going to use memory wire you must invest in these; the wire will damage standard cutters.